We hope this book helps you as you start this new phase in your life

Menstruals & Menses

Paperback ISBN: 9798757967066

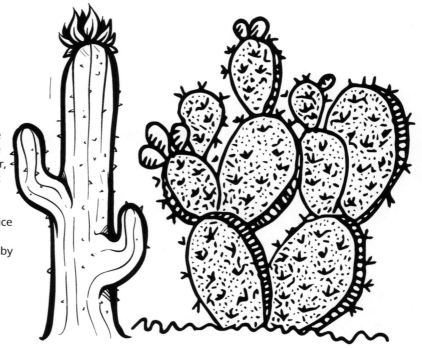

Starting your Period.....

Starting your period can be a big change! These changes in your body can bring lots of questions and concerns. You may wonder, "Why is this happening?" or "Will this ever go away?" You may also be worried about accidents at school, with friends, or in a public place. Good news! This book was created to help you understand your body and prevent accidents. Overtime, handling your period will become second-nature and a part of your monthly routine. You got this !

The Menstrual Cycle & Your Period

Your period is a part of the menstrual cycle. A menstrual cycle is a series of hormonal changes in your body that are repeated each month. It is a part of getting older and growing into a beautiful young woman. A average menstrual cycle is 28 days but it can be shorter or longer depending on the person. Your period starts at the beginning of each menstrual cycle. A period is when the lining of the uterus, a organ in your body, sheds, breaks down, and bleeds. You typically get your period at the end of puberty.

A average menstrual cycle length is 28 days but this can can vary from person to person. In order to find your average menstrual cycle length, it is important to track your cycle for at least 4 months (3 cycles) in this book if you have just started your period, or if you have just started tracking your period.

Remember 28 days is only a average

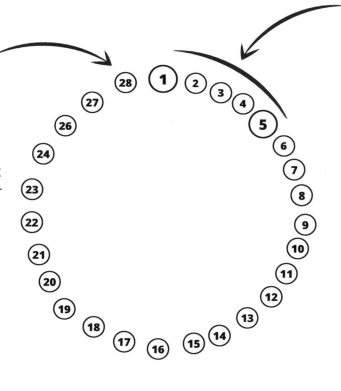

Your period happens at the start of your menstrual cycle. It typically last 3-5 days. However, a period length can vary from person to person. It can be shorter or longer. It is important to record when your period starts and ends in this book in order to know your own average period length.

Remember 3 - 5 days is only a average

What To Expect with Each Period?
Symptoms, Body Changes, Period Length, Blood Flow

Noticing changes in your body during or before your period is normal because of the hormonal changes that are happening inside of you. You may or may not experience these changes and symptoms.

Common Symptoms

- Sore Breast
- Cramps
- Headaches
- Bloating
- Acne

Common Changes

- Energy Levels
- Mood

You may find that your period may be longer or shorter each month. You may also find that the amount of blood you bleed during your period is different each day. This is normal. Overtime you will come to know your own average period length and blood flow.

Period Length

Period length is how long you bleed. Each person's period varies in length. Your best friend's period may be 3 days while yours may be 2 , 5, or 7 days. It is important to know how long your period last so you can know what to expect each month.

Blood Flow

Blood flow is the the amount of blood that is released during your period. The amount of blood at the beginning, middle, and end of your period can vary. You may have a lighter flow of blood at the start of your period (day 1) , a heavier flow in the middle (day 2 or 3), and a lighter flow toward the end (day 3, 4, or 5). It is important to know what days during your period that you bleed more or less.

WHY IS TRACKING YOUR PERIOD, SYMPTOMS, BODY CHANGES, & BLOOD FLOW IMPORTANT?

Being aware of when your period starts and ends, symptoms, body changes you experience during your period, and your period length will help you to better plan and prepare for the days that you bleed. Planning and preparing can help you to prevent accidents or disappointments. For example, you can prepare by having tampons, pads, or a menstrual cup before the start of your period so you will not have a accident. You can plan to do activities when you know you will not have cramps and low energy. While tracking, if you find that you experience headaches each month, you can prepare to have pain medication in your bag. If you and your friends would like to go to the beach, you can plan to go to the beach on the day that your period is not expected to start. Overtime, tracking your period and other body changes will become second-nature. You got this !

Step 1: Find Your Menstrual cycle length

To know when your period starts each month, you must first know your average menstrual cycle length

How can I find my average menstrual cycle length?

Start on the 1st day of your last period and count out the number of days to the 1st day of your current period. This is the length of your menstrual cycle. Do this for at least 3 cycles or 4 months. After 4 months of tracking, add up your past 3 menstrual cycle lengths and divide the total amount by 3 to get your average menstrual cycle length.

Example:

1st day of last period: August 22nd
Menstrual cycle length: 25 days

1st day of current period: September 15th

1st day of last period: September 15th
Menstrual cycle length: 28 days

1st day of current period: October 12th

1st day of last period: October 12th
Menstrual cycle length: 27 days

1st day of current period: November 7th

Average menstrual cycle length:

25 + 28 + 27 = 79   79/3= 26.3 or About 26 to 27 days

What if this is my first period or first time tracking my period ?

If this is your first period or first time tracking your period, let's just say your average menstrual cycle length is 28 days for now until you have a average of your own.

Step 2: Count Out The Number of Days in your average menstrual cycle BY Starting on The First Day of your Last Period

Grab a calendar and start on the first day of your last period and count out the number of days in your average menstrual cycle. The date on the calendar that you land on is when your period is most likely to start!

Remember, If you have just started your period, or if this your first time tracking your period, start on the day that your period started and use a 28 day average menstrual cycle length as a estimate.

If you do not remember your last period start date, estimate the start date of your last period as best as you can.

Susie just started her period on October 25th and she wants to know when her next period will start. She knows that in order to calculate her next period she first must know her average menstrual cycle length. Susie does not know her average menstrual cycle length because this is her first period. However, she knows that the average menstrual cycle is 28 days long. She uses this as base line to determine her next period. She counts 28 days from the day her period started. She lands on November 21st. Susie's period is expected to start around November 21st.

*Susie is mindful that 28 days is a average menstrual cycle length, so she plans to have all her period essentials leading up to November 21st. She will continue to track her period over the next 4 months (3 cycles), so she can have a personalized average menstrual cycle length that can help her better determine when her period will start each month.

October 2021

SUN	MON	TUE	WED	THU	FRI	SAT
26	27	28	29	30	1	2
3	4	5	6	7	8	9
10	11	12	13	14	15	16
17	18	19	20	21	22	23
24	**25**	26	27	28	29	30
31						

Novmeber 2021

SUN	MON	TUE	WED	THU	FRI	SAT
	1	2	3	4	5	6
7	8	9	10	11	12	13
14	15	16	17	18	19	20
21	22	23	24	25	26	27
28	29	30	1	2	3	4

Help Katie Find Out When Her Period Is Expected to Start Next Month

After 4 months of tracking her period Katie realized her menstrual cycle is about 21 days long. Her last period started on October the 12th and lasted for about 3 days.

What date next month is her period expected to start?
What is the expected length of Katie's next period?

October 2021

SUN	MON	TUE	WED	THU	FRI	SAT
26	27	28	29	30	1	2
3	4	5	6	7	8	9
10	11	**12**	13	14	15	16
17	18	19	20	21	22	23
24	25	26	27	28	29	30
31						

November 2021

SUN	MON	TUE	WED	THU	FRI	SAT
	1	2	3	4	5	6
7	8	9	10	11	12	13
14	15	16	17	18	19	20
21	22	23	24	25	26	27
28	29	30	1	2	3	4

Answer: Katie's period is expected to start on November 1, 2021 and it is expected to last 3 days

Ally just got her first period on October 17th, so she does not know what her average menstrual cycle. She finds that the average menstrual cycle is about 28 days, so she uses that information to give her idea of when her next period is going to come on.

What date next month is her period expected to start?

October 2021

SUN	MON	TUE	WED	THU	FRI	SAT
26	27	28	29	30	1	2
3	4	5	6	7	8	9
10	11	12	13	14	15	16
17	18	19	20	21	22	23
24	25	26	27	28	29	30
31						

Novmeber 2021

SUN	MON	TUE	WED	THU	FRI	SAT
	1	2	3	4	5	6
7	8	9	10	11	12	13
14	15	16	17	18	19	20
21	22	23	24	25	26	27
28	29	30	1	2	3	4

Answer: Ally's period is expected to start on November 13th, 2021

HOW TO USE THIS BOOK

1. Circle and record the day your period begins on the calendar each month
2. Circle symptoms, blood flow, mood, and energy levels in the daily log each day of your period. Write down any notes you may have as well.
3. Repeat steps 1-2 each day of your period until your period ends
4. On the last day of your period, go to the calendar to write the day your period ended, how long it lasted, your menstrual cycle length, and your next expected period

Note on Menstrual Length

If you have just started your period, leave the menstrual cycle length area blank for now. Begin recording your menstrual cycle length next month.

Note on Next Expected Period

If you have just started your period, use 28 days as a base line to find when your next period is most likely to start. You will have a better idea of your menstrual cycle length on you next period.

Reminder

Knowing a average length of your menstrual cycle will help you to have a more accurate estimate of your next period. Remember, to find your average menstrual cycle length track your period for at least 3 cycles (3 to 4 months). Add up your menstrual cycle lengths from the past 3 cycles and divide by 3 to get a average of the length of your menstrual cycle.

It's important to note that tracking your period can only give you a estimate of when your period will mostly likely start. If your period is irregular, this can effect your tracking results.

Daily Log Sections & Definitions

With each period you will be tracking your symptoms, blood flow, mood, and energy level

Symptoms

- **Cramps:** sharp or dull pain in your stomach
- **Headache:** sharp or dull throbbing pain in your head
- **Bloating**: feeling full as if you have already ate
- **Acne:** small bumps that may be filled with puss that may appear on your face or other parts of your body
- **Sore breast:** feeling a dull pain when you touch your breast

Blood Flow

- **Really light:** little to no blood
- **Light:** a little bit of blood
- **Medium:** a good bit of blood
- **Heavy:** a lot of blood
- **Really heavy:** a lot of blood that causes you have to change your pad, tampon, or menstrual cup every hour

Daily Log Sections & Definitions

Mood

A mood is feeling a certain way for a long period of time (more than a hour). In each log, you can circle whether you feel sad, cranky, irritable, annoyed, happy, frustrated, or tired. You can write any other feeling you may have in mind as well.

- **Sad:** feeling unhappy
- **Cranky:** you may feel like you do not want to bothered by anyone, you may complain more than usual, and every small things may bother you
- **Irritable:** you may feel easily upset by situations that do not normally bother you
- **Annoyed:** feeling upset by something that you do not like more than you usually do
- **Happy:** feeling good inside and and sometimes excited and joyful
- **Frustrated:** feeling angry or upset at something you do not like
- **Tired:** you may find it hard to get up and do things you would normally do and you may only want to sleep and stay in bed

Energy Level

Your energy level is how much you feel like doing a activity or task

- **Low:** you may feel that you do not want to do anything except sleep and rest
- **Medium:** you may feel fine being able to do simple activities where you do not have to put in a lot of effort, but you may get tired after a short period of time
- **High:** you may feel great and like your normal yourself

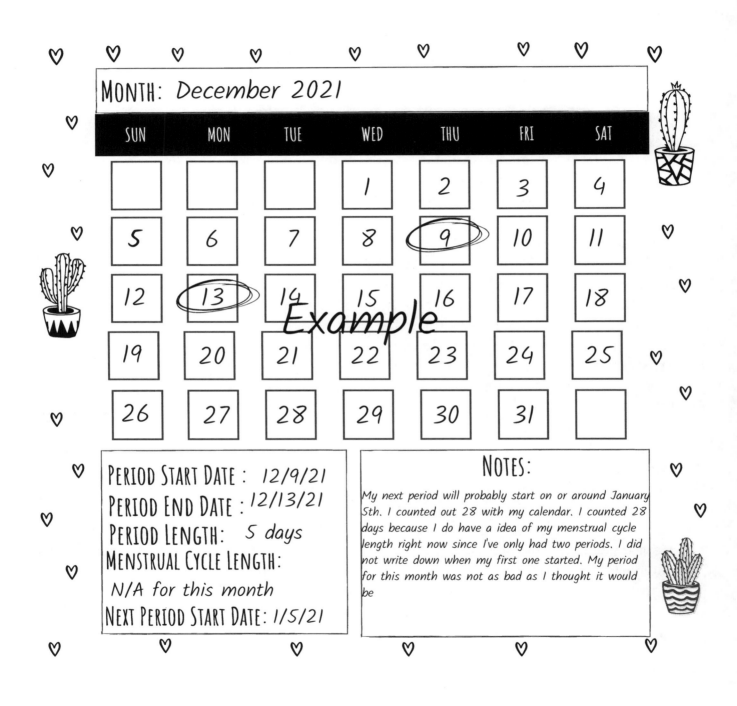

MONTH: *December 2021*

SUN	MON	TUE	WED	THU	FRI	SAT
			1	2	3	4
5	6	7	8	9	10	11
12	13	14	15	16	17	18
19	20	21	22	23	24	25
26	27	28	29	30	31	

Example

PERIOD START DATE : 12/9/21
PERIOD END DATE : 12/13/21
PERIOD LENGTH: 5 days
MENSTRUAL CYCLE LENGTH:
N/A for this month
NEXT PERIOD START DATE: 1/5/21

NOTES:

My next period will probably start on or around January 5th. I counted out 28 with my calendar. I counted 28 days because I do have a idea of my menstrual cycle length right now since I've only had two periods. I did not write down when my first one started. My period for this month was not as bad as I thought it would be

DATE: December 9, 2021

MOOD: Sad *(Cranky)* *(Irritable)* Annoyed Happy Frustrated *(Tired)* Other:

SYMPTOMS: *(Cramps)* Sore Breast Headache Acne Bloating Other:

ENERGY *(Low)* Medium High

BLOOD FLOW: Really Light *(Light)* Medium Heavy Really Heavy

NOTES:

I fell asleep and slept longer than I usually do with my naps. I was pretty cranky today too. I started to have some cramps when I got home from school so I asked my mom for some medicine

Example

DATE: December 10, 2021

MOOD: Sad Cranky Irritable Annoyed Happy Frustrated Tired Other: *I feel like myself*

SYMPTOMS: Cramps Sore Breast Headache Acne Bloating Other:

ENERGY *(Low)* Medium High

BLOOD FLOW: Really Light *(Light)* Medium Heavy Really Heavy

NOTES:

I wasn't as tired today but PT was not that great. I noticed I did not have as much energy to do our run like I usually do.

DATE: December 11, 2021

MOOD: Sad Cranky Irritable Annoyed Happy Frustrated Tired Other:

SYMPTOMS: Cramps Sore Breast Headache Acne Bloating Other:

ENERGY Low (Medium) High

BLOOD FLOW: Really Light Light (Medium) Heavy Really Heavy

NOTES:

I noticed there was more blood today than the days earlier in the week. I packed some extra pads in my backpack for school

Example

DATE: December 12, 2021

MOOD: Sad Cranky Irritable Annoyed Happy Frustrated Tired Other:

SYMPTOMS: Cramps Sore Breast Headache Acne Bloating Other:

ENERGY Low (Medium) High

BLOOD FLOW: Really Light Light (Medium) Heavy Really Heavy

NOTES:

My bleeding was still medium today. I'm so glad I packed extra pads in case I ran out !

DATE: December 13, 2021

MOOD: Sad Cranky Irritable Annoyed Happy Frustrated Tired Other:

SYMPTOMS: Cramps Sore Breast Headache Acne Bloating Other:

ENERGY Low Medium (High)

BLOOD FLOW: Really Light (Light) Medium Heavy Really Heavy

NOTES:

There was not much in my pad today but light spots.
I am feeling more like myself.

Example

DATE: December 14, 2021

MOOD: Sad Cranky Irritable Annoyed Happy Frustrated Tired Other:

SYMPTOMS: Cramps Sore Breast Headache Acne Bloating Other:

ENERGY Low Medium (High)

BLOOD FLOW: Really Light Light Medium Heavy Really Heavy

NOTES:

I think my period is off now. I didn't really see anything in my pad.
I am back to my normal self !

You Got This !

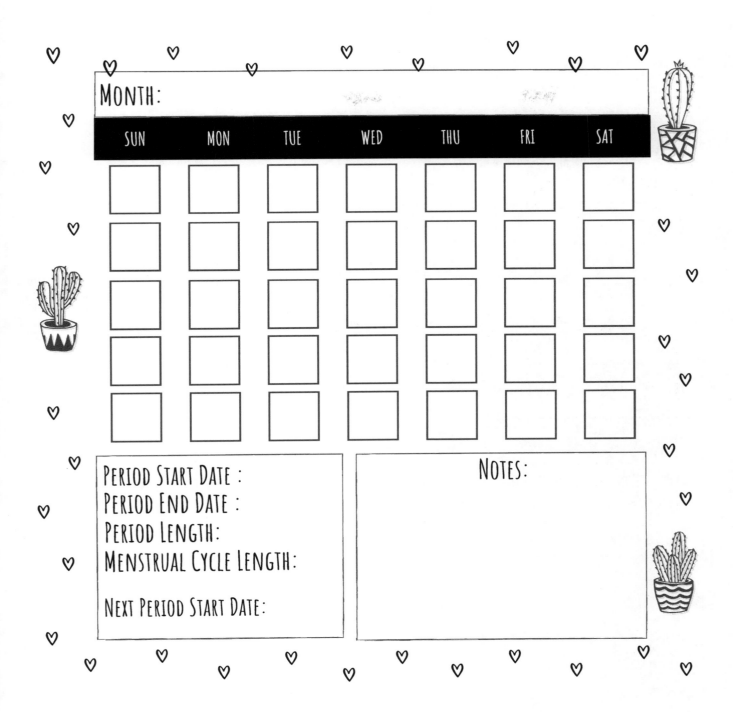

MONTH:

SUN	MON	TUE	WED	THU	FRI	SAT

PERIOD START DATE :
PERIOD END DATE :
PERIOD LENGTH:
MENSTRUAL CYCLE LENGTH:

NEXT PERIOD START DATE:

NOTES:

Date:

Mood: Sad Cranky Irritable Annoyed Happy Frustrated Tired Other:

Symptoms: Cramps Sore Breast Headache Acne Bloating Other:

Energy Low Medium High

Blood Flow: Really Light Light Medium Heavy Really Heavy

Notes

Date:

Mood: Sad Cranky Irritable Annoyed Happy Frustrated Tired Other:

Symptoms: Cramps Sore Breast Headache Acne Bloating Other:

Energy Low Medium High

Blood Flow: Really Light Light Medium Heavy Really Heavy

Notes

Date:

Mood: Sad   Cranky   Irritable   Annoyed   Happy   Frustrated   Tired   Other:

Symptoms: Cramps   Sore Breast   Headache   Acne   Bloating   Other:

Energy   Low   Medium   High

Blood Flow: Really Light   Light   Medium   Heavy   Really Heavy

Notes

Date:

Mood: Sad   Cranky   Irritable   Annoyed   Happy   Frustrated   Tired   Other:

Symptoms: Cramps   Sore Breast   Headache   Acne   Bloating   Other:

Energy   Low   Medium   High

Blood Flow: Really Light   Light   Medium   Heavy   Really Heavy

Notes

Date:

Mood: Sad Cranky Irritable Annoyed Happy Frustrated Tired Other:

Symptoms: Cramps Sore Breast Headache Acne Bloating Other:

Energy Low Medium High

Blood Flow: Really Light Light Medium Heavy Really Heavy

Notes

Date:

Mood: Sad Cranky Irritable Annoyed Happy Frustrated Tired Other:

Symptoms: Cramps Sore Breast Headache Acne Bloating Other:

Energy Low Medium High

Blood Flow: Really Light Light Medium Heavy Really Heavy

Notes

Don't Stop Keep Tracking !

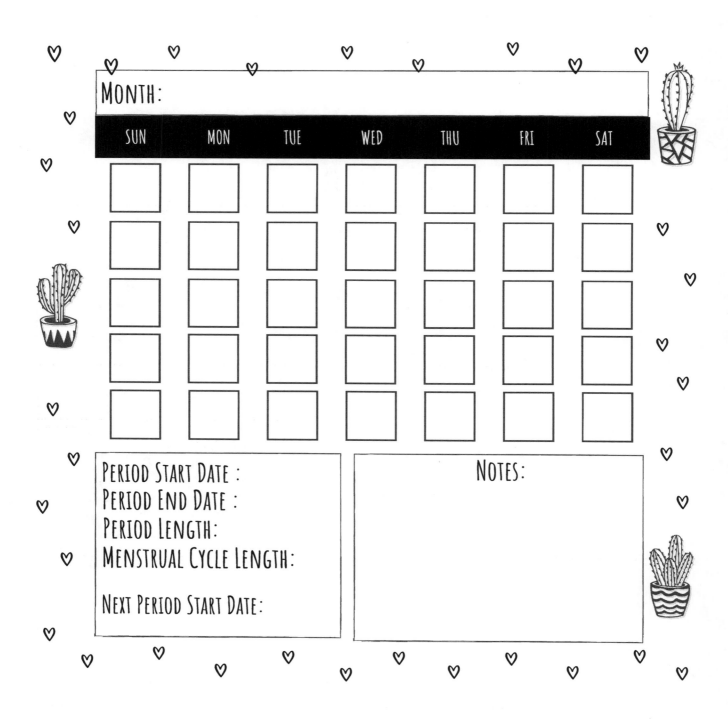

MONTH:

SUN	MON	TUE	WED	THU	FRI	SAT

PERIOD START DATE :
PERIOD END DATE :
PERIOD LENGTH:
MENSTRUAL CYCLE LENGTH:

NEXT PERIOD START DATE:

NOTES:

DATE:

MOOD: Sad Cranky Irritable Annoyed Happy Frustrated Tired Other:

SYMPTOMS: Cramps Sore Breast Headache Acne Bloating Other:

ENERGY Low Medium High

BLOOD FLOW: Really Light Light Medium Heavy Really Heavy

NOTES

DATE:

MOOD: Sad Cranky Irritable Annoyed Happy Frustrated Tired Other:

SYMPTOMS: Cramps Sore Breast Headache Acne Bloating Other:

ENERGY Low Medium High

BLOOD FLOW: Really Light Light Medium Heavy Really Heavy

NOTES

Date:

Mood: Sad Cranky Irritable Annoyed Happy Frustrated Tired Other:

Symptoms: Cramps Sore Breast Headache Acne Bloating Other:

Energy Low Medium High

Blood Flow: Really Light Light Medium Heavy Really Heavy

Notes

Date:

Mood: Sad Cranky Irritable Annoyed Happy Frustrated Tired Other:

Symptoms: Cramps Sore Breast Headache Acne Bloating Other:

Energy Low Medium High

Blood Flow: Really Light Light Medium Heavy Really Heavy

Notes

DATE:

MOOD: Sad   Cranky   Irritable   Annoyed   Happy   Frustrated   Tired   Other:

SYMPTOMS: Cramps   Sore Breast   Headache   Acne   Bloating   Other:

ENERGY   Low   Medium   High

BLOOD FLOW: Really Light   Light   Medium   Heavy   Really Heavy

NOTES

DATE:

MOOD: Sad   Cranky   Irritable   Annoyed   Happy   Frustrated   Tired   Other:

SYMPTOMS: Cramps   Sore Breast   Headache   Acne   Bloating   Other:

ENERGY   Low   Medium   High

BLOOD FLOW: Really Light   Light   Medium   Heavy   Really Heavy

NOTES

DATE:

MOOD: Sad Cranky Irritable Annoyed Happy Frustrated Tired Other:

SYMPTOMS: Cramps Sore Breast Headache Acne Bloating Other:

ENERGY Low Medium High

BLOOD FLOW: Really Light Light Medium Heavy Really Heavy

NOTES

DATE:

MOOD: Sad Cranky Irritable Annoyed Happy Frustrated Tired Other:

SYMPTOMS: Cramps Sore Breast Headache Acne Bloating Other:

ENERGY Low Medium High

BLOOD FLOW: Really Light Light Medium Heavy Really Heavy

NOTES

You Made it to Month 3 Keep it up!

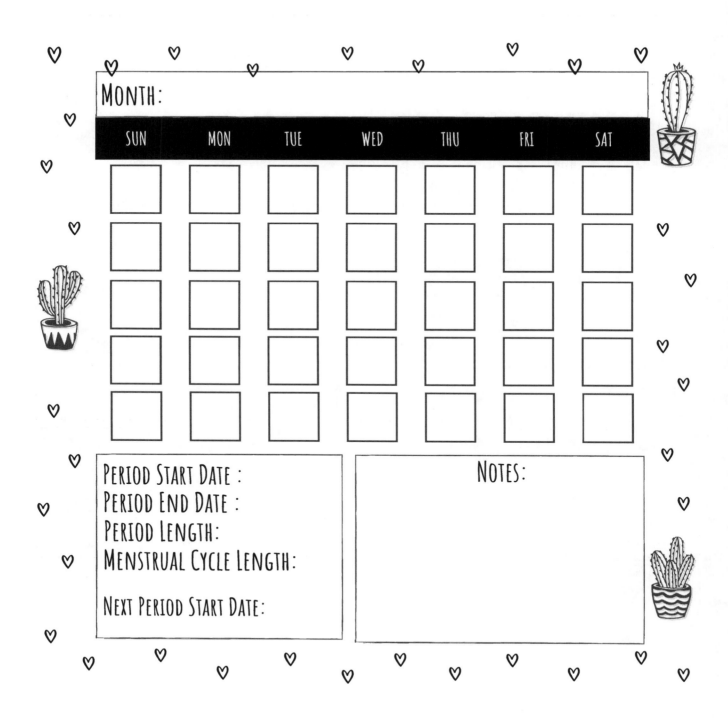

MONTH:

SUN	MON	TUE	WED	THU	FRI	SAT

PERIOD START DATE :
PERIOD END DATE :
PERIOD LENGTH:
MENSTRUAL CYCLE LENGTH:

NEXT PERIOD START DATE:

NOTES:

Date:

Mood: Sad Cranky Irritable Annoyed Happy Frustrated Tired Other:

Symptoms: Cramps Sore Breast Headache Acne Bloating Other:

Energy Low Medium High

Blood Flow: Really Light Light Medium Heavy Really Heavy

Notes

Date:

Mood: Sad Cranky Irritable Annoyed Happy Frustrated Tired Other:

Symptoms: Cramps Sore Breast Headache Acne Bloating Other:

Energy Low Medium High

Blood Flow: Really Light Light Medium Heavy Really Heavy

Notes

DATE:

MOOD: Sad Cranky Irritable Annoyed Happy Frustrated Tired Other:

SYMPTOMS: Cramps Sore Breast Headache Acne Bloating Other:

ENERGY Low Medium High

BLOOD FLOW: Really Light Light Medium Heavy Really Heavy

NOTES

DATE:

MOOD: Sad Cranky Irritable Annoyed Happy Frustrated Tired Other:

SYMPTOMS: Cramps Sore Breast Headache Acne Bloating Other:

ENERGY Low Medium High

BLOOD FLOW: Really Light Light Medium Heavy Really Heavy

NOTES

Date:

Mood: Sad Cranky Irritable Annoyed Happy Frustrated Tired Other:

Symptoms: Cramps Sore Breast Headache Acne Bloating Other:

Energy Low Medium High

Blood Flow: Really Light Light Medium Heavy Really Heavy

Notes

Date:

Mood: Sad Cranky Irritable Annoyed Happy Frustrated Tired Other:

Symptoms: Cramps Sore Breast Headache Acne Bloating Other:

Energy Low Medium High

Blood Flow: Really Light Light Medium Heavy Really Heavy

Notes

Date:

Mood: Sad Cranky Irritable Annoyed Happy Frustrated Tired Other:

Symptoms: Cramps Sore Breast Headache Acne Bloating Other:

Energy Low Medium High

Blood Flow: Really Light Light Medium Heavy Really Heavy

Notes

Date:

Mood: Sad Cranky Irritable Annoyed Happy Frustrated Tired Other:

Symptoms: Cramps Sore Breast Headache Acne Bloating Other:

Energy Low Medium High

Blood Flow: Really Light Light Medium Heavy Really Heavy

Notes

Hooray !
4 Months of tracking
3 cycles. Now you have
your Average
Menstrual Cycle
Length. Don't Stop,
Keep Recording !

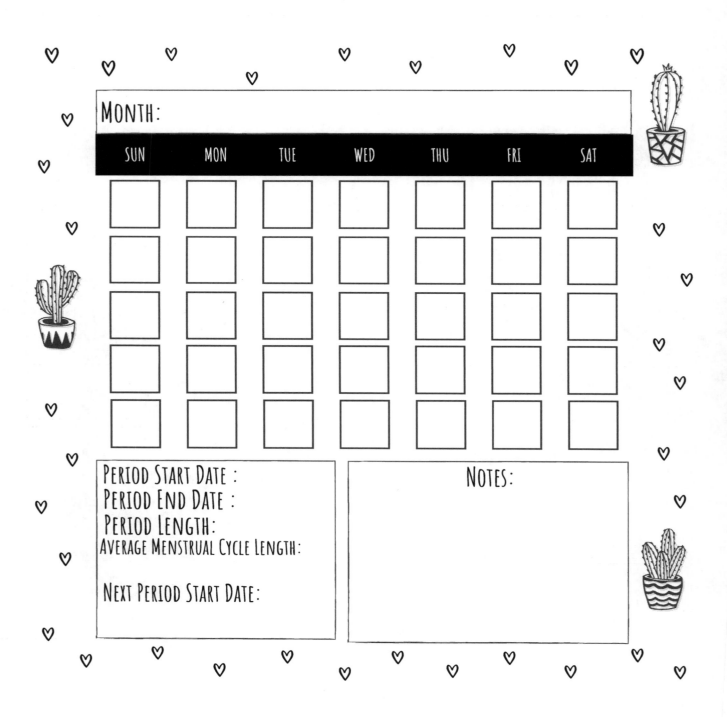

Month:

SUN	MON	TUE	WED	THU	FRI	SAT

Period Start Date :
Period End Date :
Period Length:
Average Menstrual Cycle Length:

Next Period Start Date:

Notes:

Date:

Mood: Sad Cranky Irritable Annoyed Happy Frustrated Tired Other:

Symptoms: Cramps Sore Breast Headache Acne Bloating Other:

Energy Low Medium High

Blood Flow: Really Light Light Medium Heavy Really Heavy

Notes

Date:

Mood: Sad Cranky Irritable Annoyed Happy Frustrated Tired Other:

Symptoms: Cramps Sore Breast Headache Acne Bloating Other:

Energy Low Medium High

Blood Flow: Really Light Light Medium Heavy Really Heavy

Notes

DATE:

MOOD: Sad Cranky Irritable Annoyed Happy Frustrated Tired Other:

SYMPTOMS: Cramps Sore Breast Headache Acne Bloating Other:

ENERGY Low Medium High

BLOOD FLOW: Really Light Light Medium Heavy Really Heavy

NOTES

DATE:

MOOD: Sad Cranky Irritable Annoyed Happy Frustrated Tired Other:

SYMPTOMS: Cramps Sore Breast Headache Acne Bloating Other:

ENERGY Low Medium High

BLOOD FLOW: Really Light Light Medium Heavy Really Heavy

NOTES

Date:

Mood: Sad Cranky Irritable Annoyed Happy Frustrated Tired Other:

Symptoms: Cramps Sore Breast Headache Acne Bloating Other:

Energy Low Medium High

Blood Flow: Really Light Light Medium Heavy Really Heavy

Notes

Date:

Mood: Sad Cranky Irritable Annoyed Happy Frustrated Tired Other:

Symptoms: Cramps Sore Breast Headache Acne Bloating Other:

Energy Low Medium High

Blood Flow: Really Light Light Medium Heavy Really Heavy

Notes

DATE:

MOOD: Sad Cranky Irritable Annoyed Happy Frustrated Tired Other:

SYMPTOMS: Cramps Sore Breast Headache Acne Bloating Other:

ENERGY Low Medium High

BLOOD FLOW: Really Light Light Medium Heavy Really Heavy

NOTES

DATE:

MOOD: Sad Cranky Irritable Annoyed Happy Frustrated Tired Other:

SYMPTOMS: Cramps Sore Breast Headache Acne Bloating Other:

ENERGY Low Medium High

BLOOD FLOW: Really Light Light Medium Heavy Really Heavy

NOTES

You ARE Awesome !

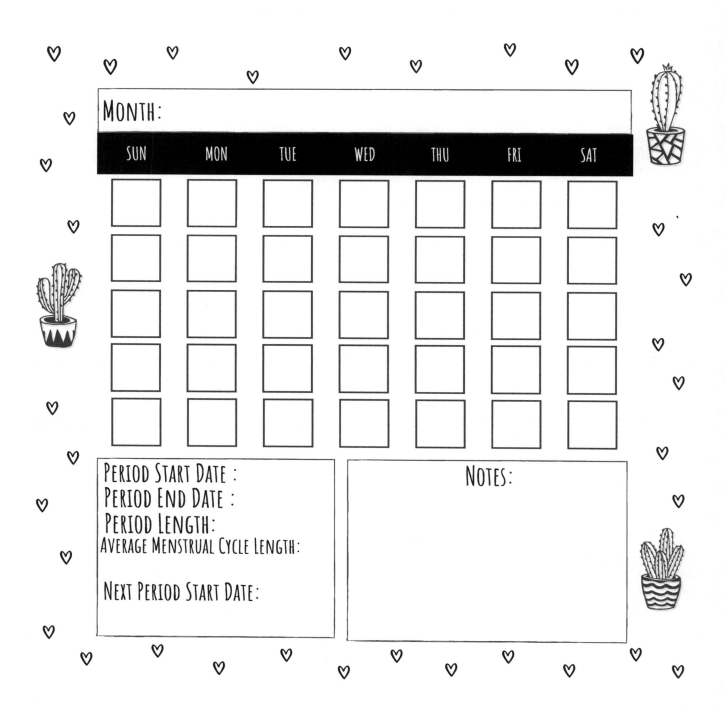

MONTH:

SUN	MON	TUE	WED	THU	FRI	SAT

PERIOD START DATE :
PERIOD END DATE :
PERIOD LENGTH:
AVERAGE MENSTRUAL CYCLE LENGTH:

NEXT PERIOD START DATE:

NOTES:

DATE:

MOOD: Sad Cranky Irritable Annoyed Happy Frustrated Tired Other:

SYMPTOMS: Cramps Sore Breast Headache Acne Bloating Other:

ENERGY Low Medium High

BLOOD FLOW: Really Light Light Medium Heavy Really Heavy

NOTES

DATE:

MOOD: Sad Cranky Irritable Annoyed Happy Frustrated Tired Other:

SYMPTOMS: Cramps Sore Breast Headache Acne Bloating Other:

ENERGY Low Medium High

BLOOD FLOW: Really Light Light Medium Heavy Really Heavy

NOTES

Date:

Mood: Sad Cranky Irritable Annoyed Happy Frustrated Tired Other:

Symptoms: Cramps Sore Breast Headache Acne Bloating Other:

Energy Low Medium High

Blood Flow: Really Light Light Medium Heavy Really Heavy

Notes

Date:

Mood: Sad Cranky Irritable Annoyed Happy Frustrated Tired Other:

Symptoms: Cramps Sore Breast Headache Acne Bloating Other:

Energy Low Medium High

Blood Flow: Really Light Light Medium Heavy Really Heavy

Notes

DATE:

MOOD: Sad Cranky Irritable Annoyed Happy Frustrated Tired Other:

SYMPTOMS: Cramps Sore Breast Headache Acne Bloating Other:

ENERGY Low Medium High

BLOOD FLOW: Really Light Light Medium Heavy Really Heavy

NOTES

DATE:

MOOD: Sad Cranky Irritable Annoyed Happy Frustrated Tired Other:

SYMPTOMS: Cramps Sore Breast Headache Acne Bloating Other:

ENERGY Low Medium High

BLOOD FLOW: Really Light Light Medium Heavy Really Heavy

NOTES

Date:

Mood: Sad Cranky Irritable Annoyed Happy Frustrated Tired Other:

Symptoms: Cramps Sore Breast Headache Acne Bloating Other:

Energy Low Medium High

Blood Flow: Really Light Light Medium Heavy Really Heavy

Notes

Date:

Mood: Sad Cranky Irritable Annoyed Happy Frustrated Tired Other:

Symptoms: Cramps Sore Breast Headache Acne Bloating Other:

Energy Low Medium High

Blood Flow: Really Light Light Medium Heavy Really Heavy

Notes

YOU ARE DOING A GREAT JOB !

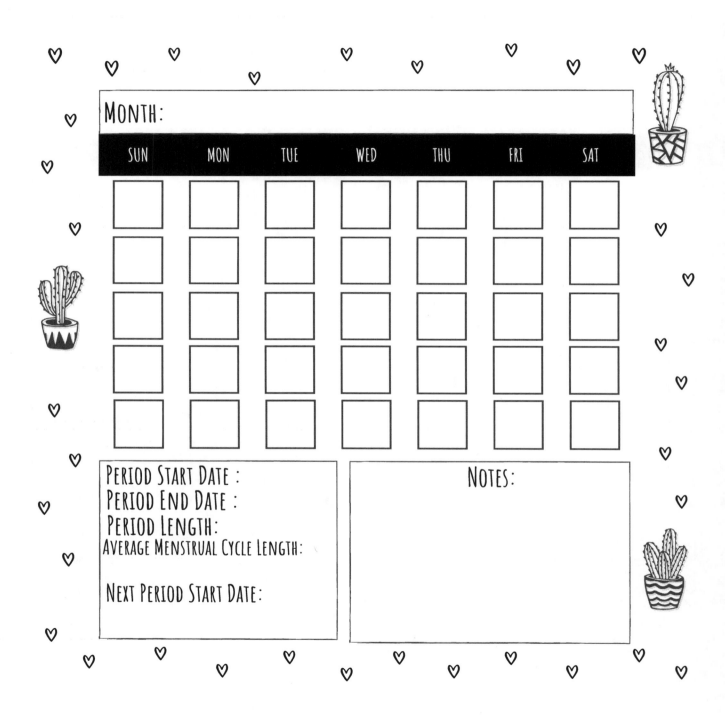

MONTH:

SUN	MON	TUE	WED	THU	FRI	SAT

PERIOD START DATE :
PERIOD END DATE :
PERIOD LENGTH:
AVERAGE MENSTRUAL CYCLE LENGTH:

NEXT PERIOD START DATE:

NOTES:

DATE:

MOOD: Sad Cranky Irritable Annoyed Happy Frustrated Tired Other:

SYMPTOMS: Cramps Sore Breast Headache Acne Bloating Other:

ENERGY Low Medium High

BLOOD FLOW: Really Light Light Medium Heavy Really Heavy

NOTES

DATE:

MOOD: Sad Cranky Irritable Annoyed Happy Frustrated Tired Other:

SYMPTOMS: Cramps Sore Breast Headache Acne Bloating Other:

ENERGY Low Medium High

BLOOD FLOW: Really Light Light Medium Heavy Really Heavy

NOTES

DATE:

MOOD: Sad Cranky Irritable Annoyed Happy Frustrated Tired Other:

SYMPTOMS: Cramps Sore Breast Headache Acne Bloating Other:

ENERGY Low Medium High

BLOOD FLOW: Really Light Light Medium Heavy Really Heavy

NOTES

DATE:

MOOD: Sad Cranky Irritable Annoyed Happy Frustrated Tired Other:

SYMPTOMS: Cramps Sore Breast Headache Acne Bloating Other:

ENERGY Low Medium High

BLOOD FLOW: Really Light Light Medium Heavy Really Heavy

NOTES

DATE:

MOOD: Sad Cranky Irritable Annoyed Happy Frustrated Tired Other:

SYMPTOMS: Cramps Sore Breast Headache Acne Bloating Other:

ENERGY Low Medium High

BLOOD FLOW: Really Light Light Medium Heavy Really Heavy

NOTES

DATE:

MOOD: Sad Cranky Irritable Annoyed Happy Frustrated Tired Other:

SYMPTOMS: Cramps Sore Breast Headache Acne Bloating Other:

ENERGY Low Medium High

BLOOD FLOW: Really Light Light Medium Heavy Really Heavy

NOTES

Date:

Mood: Sad Cranky Irritable Annoyed Happy Frustrated Tired Other:

Symptoms: Cramps Sore Breast Headache Acne Bloating Other:

Energy Low Medium High

Blood Flow: Really Light Light Medium Heavy Really Heavy

Notes

Date:

Mood: Sad Cranky Irritable Annoyed Happy Frustrated Tired Other:

Symptoms: Cramps Sore Breast Headache Acne Bloating Other:

Energy Low Medium High

Blood Flow: Really Light Light Medium Heavy Really Heavy

Notes

KEEP UP THE GOOD WORK !

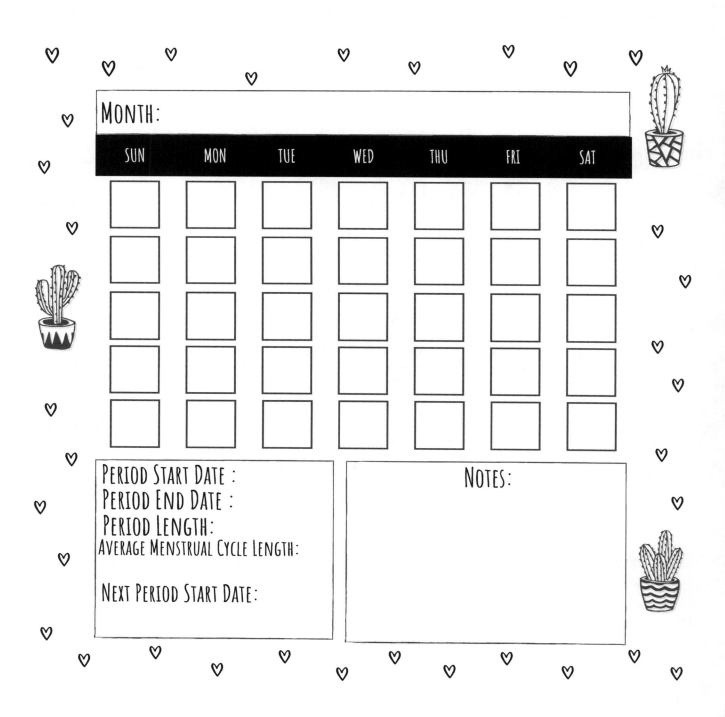

MONTH:

SUN	MON	TUE	WED	THU	FRI	SAT

PERIOD START DATE :
PERIOD END DATE :
PERIOD LENGTH:
AVERAGE MENSTRUAL CYCLE LENGTH:

NEXT PERIOD START DATE:

NOTES:

DATE:

MOOD: Sad Cranky Irritable Annoyed Happy Frustrated Tired Other:

SYMPTOMS: Cramps Sore Breast Headache Acne Bloating Other:

ENERGY Low Medium High

BLOOD FLOW: Really Light Light Medium Heavy Really Heavy

NOTES

DATE:

MOOD: Sad Cranky Irritable Annoyed Happy Frustrated Tired Other:

SYMPTOMS: Cramps Sore Breast Headache Acne Bloating Other:

ENERGY Low Medium High

BLOOD FLOW: Really Light Light Medium Heavy Really Heavy

NOTES

Date:

Mood: Sad Cranky Irritable Annoyed Happy Frustrated Tired Other:

Symptoms: Cramps Sore Breast Headache Acne Bloating Other:

Energy Low Medium High

Blood Flow: Really Light Light Medium Heavy Really Heavy

Notes

Date:

Mood: Sad Cranky Irritable Annoyed Happy Frustrated Tired Other:

Symptoms: Cramps Sore Breast Headache Acne Bloating Other:

Energy Low Medium High

Blood Flow: Really Light Light Medium Heavy Really Heavy

Notes

DATE:

MOOD: Sad Cranky Irritable Annoyed Happy Frustrated Tired Other:

SYMPTOMS: Cramps Sore Breast Headache Acne Bloating Other:

ENERGY Low Medium High

BLOOD FLOW: Really Light Light Medium Heavy Really Heavy

NOTES

DATE:

MOOD: Sad Cranky Irritable Annoyed Happy Frustrated Tired Other:

SYMPTOMS: Cramps Sore Breast Headache Acne Bloating Other:

ENERGY Low Medium High

BLOOD FLOW: Really Light Light Medium Heavy Really Heavy

NOTES

DATE:

MOOD: Sad Cranky Irritable Annoyed Happy Frustrated Tired Other:
SYMPTOMS: Cramps Sore Breast Headache Acne Bloating Other:
ENERGY Low Medium High
BLOOD FLOW: Really Light Light Medium Heavy Really Heavy

NOTES

DATE:

MOOD: Sad Cranky Irritable Annoyed Happy Frustrated Tired Other:
SYMPTOMS: Cramps Sore Breast Headache Acne Bloating Other:
ENERGY Low Medium High
BLOOD FLOW: Really Light Light Medium Heavy Really Heavy

NOTES

Don't Quit Keep On Tracking!

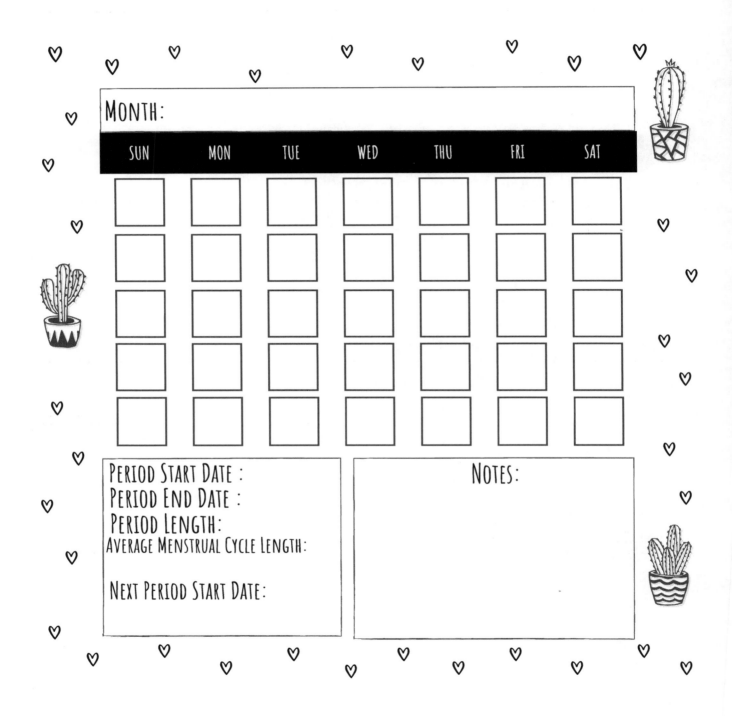

MONTH:

SUN	MON	TUE	WED	THU	FRI	SAT

PERIOD START DATE :
PERIOD END DATE :
PERIOD LENGTH:
AVERAGE MENSTRUAL CYCLE LENGTH:

NEXT PERIOD START DATE:

NOTES:

DATE:

MOOD: Sad Cranky Irritable Annoyed Happy Frustrated Tired Other:

SYMPTOMS: Cramps Sore Breast Headache Acne Bloating Other:

ENERGY Low Medium High

BLOOD FLOW: Really Light Light Medium Heavy Really Heavy

NOTES

DATE:

MOOD: Sad Cranky Irritable Annoyed Happy Frustrated Tired Other:

SYMPTOMS: Cramps Sore Breast Headache Acne Bloating Other:

ENERGY Low Medium High

BLOOD FLOW: Really Light Light Medium Heavy Really Heavy

NOTES

Date:

Mood: Sad   Cranky   Irritable   Annoyed   Happy   Frustrated   Tired   Other:

Symptoms: Cramps   Sore Breast   Headache   Acne   Bloating   Other:

Energy Low   Medium   High

Blood Flow: Really Light   Light   Medium   Heavy   Really Heavy

Notes

Date:

Mood: Sad   Cranky   Irritable   Annoyed   Happy   Frustrated   Tired   Other:

Symptoms: Cramps   Sore Breast   Headache   Acne   Bloating   Other:

Energy Low   Medium   High

Blood Flow: Really Light   Light   Medium   Heavy   Really Heavy

Notes

DATE:

MOOD: Sad Cranky Irritable Annoyed Happy Frustrated Tired Other:

SYMPTOMS: Cramps Sore Breast Headache Acne Bloating Other:

ENERGY Low Medium High

BLOOD FLOW: Really Light Light Medium Heavy Really Heavy

NOTES

DATE:

MOOD: Sad Cranky Irritable Annoyed Happy Frustrated Tired Other:

SYMPTOMS: Cramps Sore Breast Headache Acne Bloating Other:

ENERGY Low Medium High

BLOOD FLOW: Really Light Light Medium Heavy Really Heavy

NOTES

DATE:

MOOD: Sad Cranky Irritable Annoyed Happy Frustrated Tired Other:

SYMPTOMS: Cramps Sore Breast Headache Acne Bloating Other:

ENERGY Low Medium High

BLOOD FLOW: Really Light Light Medium Heavy Really Heavy

NOTES

DATE:

MOOD: Sad Cranky Irritable Annoyed Happy Frustrated Tired Other:

SYMPTOMS: Cramps Sore Breast Headache Acne Bloating Other:

ENERGY Low Medium High

BLOOD FLOW: Really Light Light Medium Heavy Really Heavy

NOTES

YOUR

BECOMING

A

PRO !

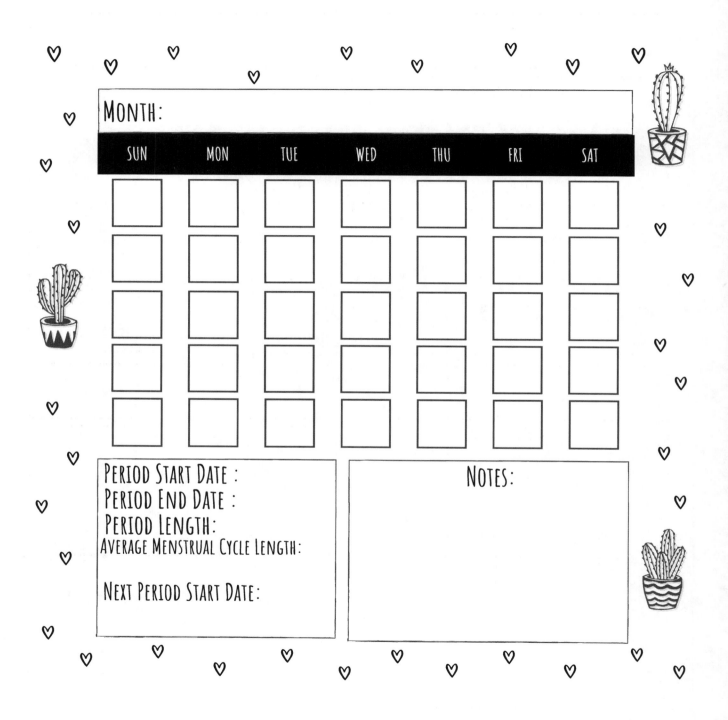

Month:

SUN	MON	TUE	WED	THU	FRI	SAT

Period Start Date :
Period End Date :
Period Length:
Average Menstrual Cycle Length:

Next Period Start Date:

Notes:

DATE:

MOOD: Sad   Cranky   Irritable   Annoyed   Happy   Frustrated   Tired   Other:

SYMPTOMS: Cramps   Sore Breast   Headache   Acne   Bloating   Other:

ENERGY   Low   Medium   High

BLOOD FLOW: Really Light   Light   Medium   Heavy   Really Heavy

NOTES

DATE:

MOOD: Sad   Cranky   Irritable   Annoyed   Happy   Frustrated   Tired   Other:

SYMPTOMS: Cramps   Sore Breast   Headache   Acne   Bloating   Other:

ENERGY   Low   Medium   High

BLOOD FLOW: Really Light   Light   Medium   Heavy   Really Heavy

NOTES

Date:

Mood: Sad Cranky Irritable Annoyed Happy Frustrated Tired Other:

Symptoms: Cramps Sore Breast Headache Acne Bloating Other:

Energy Low Medium High

Blood Flow: Really Light Light Medium Heavy Really Heavy

Notes

Date:

Mood: Sad Cranky Irritable Annoyed Happy Frustrated Tired Other:

Symptoms: Cramps Sore Breast Headache Acne Bloating Other:

Energy Low Medium High

Blood Flow: Really Light Light Medium Heavy Really Heavy

Notes

DATE:

MOOD: Sad Cranky Irritable Annoyed Happy Frustrated Tired Other:

SYMPTOMS: Cramps Sore Breast Headache Acne Bloating Other:

ENERGY   Low Medium High

BLOOD FLOW: Really Light Light Medium Heavy Really Heavy

NOTES

DATE:

MOOD: Sad Cranky Irritable Annoyed Happy Frustrated Tired Other:

SYMPTOMS: Cramps Sore Breast Headache Acne Bloating Other:

ENERGY   Low Medium High

BLOOD FLOW: Really Light Light Medium Heavy Really Heavy

NOTES

DATE:

MOOD: Sad   Cranky   Irritable   Annoyed   Happy   Frustrated   Tired   Other:

SYMPTOMS: Cramps   Sore Breast   Headache   Acne   Bloating   Other:

ENERGY   Low   Medium   High

BLOOD FLOW: Really Light   Light   Medium   Heavy   Really Heavy

NOTES

DATE:

MOOD: Sad   Cranky   Irritable   Annoyed   Happy   Frustrated   Tired   Other:

SYMPTOMS: Cramps   Sore Breast   Headache   Acne   Bloating   Other:

ENERGY   Low   Medium   High

BLOOD FLOW: Really Light   Light   Medium   Heavy   Really Heavy

NOTES

KEEP
TRACKING !

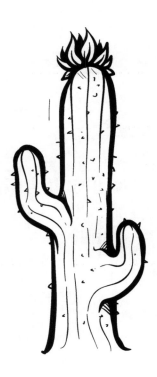

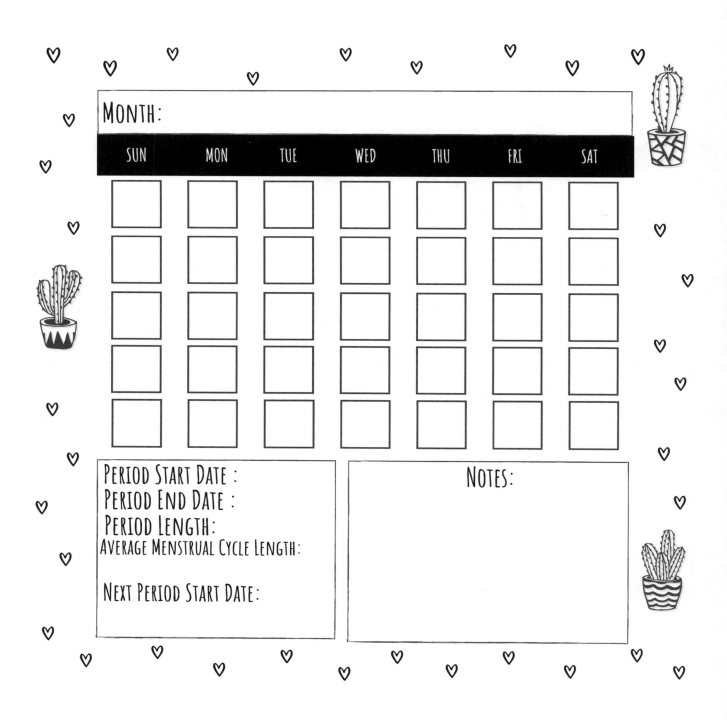

MONTH:

SUN	MON	TUE	WED	THU	FRI	SAT

PERIOD START DATE :
PERIOD END DATE :
PERIOD LENGTH:
AVERAGE MENSTRUAL CYCLE LENGTH:

NEXT PERIOD START DATE:

NOTES:

Date:

Mood: Sad Cranky Irritable Annoyed Happy Frustrated Tired Other:

Symptoms: Cramps Sore Breast Headache Acne Bloating Other:

Energy Low Medium High

Blood Flow: Really Light Light Medium Heavy Really Heavy

Notes

Date:

Mood: Sad Cranky Irritable Annoyed Happy Frustrated Tired Other:

Symptoms: Cramps Sore Breast Headache Acne Bloating Other:

Energy Low Medium High

Blood Flow: Really Light Light Medium Heavy Really Heavy

Notes

DATE:

MOOD: Sad Cranky Irritable Annoyed Happy Frustrated Tired Other:

Symptoms: Cramps Sore Breast Headache Acne Bloating Other:

Energy Low Medium High

Blood Flow: Really Light Light Medium Heavy Really Heavy

Notes

DATE:

MOOD: Sad Cranky Irritable Annoyed Happy Frustrated Tired Other:

Symptoms: Cramps Sore Breast Headache Acne Bloating Other:

Energy Low Medium High

Blood Flow: Really Light Light Medium Heavy Really Heavy

Notes

DATE:

MOOD: Sad   Cranky   Irritable   Annoyed   Happy   Frustrated   Tired   Other:

SYMPTOMS: Cramps   Sore Breast   Headache   Acne   Bloating   Other:

ENERGY   Low   Medium   High

BLOOD FLOW: Really Light   Light   Medium   Heavy   Really Heavy

NOTES

DATE:

MOOD: Sad   Cranky   Irritable   Annoyed   Happy   Frustrated   Tired   Other:

SYMPTOMS: Cramps   Sore Breast   Headache   Acne   Bloating   Other:

ENERGY   Low   Medium   High

BLOOD FLOW: Really Light   Light   Medium   Heavy   Really Heavy

NOTES

DATE:

MOOD: SAD CRANKY IRRITABLE ANNOYED HAPPY FRUSTRATED TIRED OTHER:

SYMPTOMS: CRAMPS SORE BREAST HEADACHE ACNE BLOATING OTHER:

ENERGY LOW MEDIUM HIGH

BLOOD FLOW: REALLY LIGHT LIGHT MEDIUM HEAVY REALLY HEAVY

NOTES

DATE:

MOOD: SAD CRANKY IRRITABLE ANNOYED HAPPY FRUSTRATED TIRED OTHER:

SYMPTOMS: CRAMPS SORE BREAST HEADACHE ACNE BLOATING OTHER:

ENERGY LOW MEDIUM HIGH

BLOOD FLOW: REALLY LIGHT LIGHT MEDIUM HEAVY REALLY HEAVY

NOTES

YOU HAVE DONE SUCH A GREAT JOB!

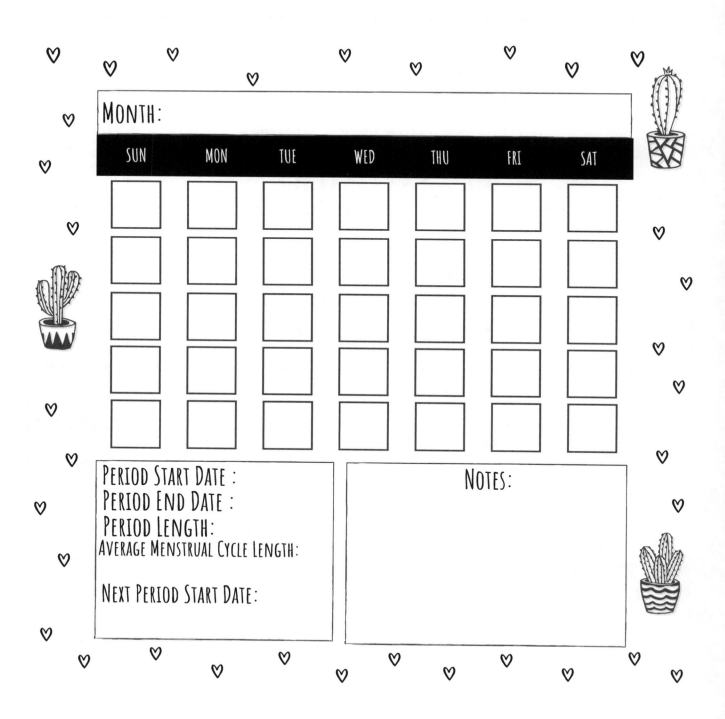

MONTH:

SUN	MON	TUE	WED	THU	FRI	SAT

PERIOD START DATE :
PERIOD END DATE :
PERIOD LENGTH:
AVERAGE MENSTRUAL CYCLE LENGTH:

NEXT PERIOD START DATE:

NOTES:

Date:

Mood: Sad Cranky Irritable Annoyed Happy Frustrated Tired Other:

Symptoms: Cramps Sore Breast Headache Acne Bloating Other:

Energy Low Medium High

Blood Flow: Really Light Light Medium Heavy Really Heavy

Notes

Date:

Mood: Sad Cranky Irritable Annoyed Happy Frustrated Tired Other:

Symptoms: Cramps Sore Breast Headache Acne Bloating Other:

Energy Low Medium High

Blood Flow: Really Light Light Medium Heavy Really Heavy

Notes

Date:

Mood: Sad Cranky Irritable Annoyed Happy Frustrated Tired Other:

Symptoms: Cramps Sore Breast Headache Acne Bloating Other:

Energy Low Medium High

Blood Flow: Really Light Light Medium Heavy Really Heavy

Notes

Date:

Mood: Sad Cranky Irritable Annoyed Happy Frustrated Tired Other:

Symptoms: Cramps Sore Breast Headache Acne Bloating Other:

Energy Low Medium High

Blood Flow: Really Light Light Medium Heavy Really Heavy

Notes

DATE:

MOOD: Sad   Cranky   Irritable   Annoyed   Happy   Frustrated   Tired   Other:

SYMPTOMS: Cramps   Sore Breast   Headache   Acne   Bloating   Other:

ENERGY   Low   Medium   High

BLOOD FLOW: Really Light   Light   Medium   Heavy   Really Heavy

---

NOTES

DATE:

MOOD: Sad   Cranky   Irritable   Annoyed   Happy   Frustrated   Tired   Other:

SYMPTOMS: Cramps   Sore Breast   Headache   Acne   Bloating   Other:

ENERGY   Low   Medium   High

BLOOD FLOW: Really Light   Light   Medium   Heavy   Really Heavy

---

NOTES

DATE:

MOOD: Sad Cranky Irritable Annoyed Happy Frustrated Tired Other:

SYMPTOMS: Cramps Sore Breast Headache Acne Bloating Other:

ENERGY Low Medium High

BLOOD FLOW: Really Light Light Medium Heavy Really Heavy

NOTES

DATE:

MOOD: Sad Cranky Irritable Annoyed Happy Frustrated Tired Other:

SYMPTOMS: Cramps Sore Breast Headache Acne Bloating Other:

ENERGY Low Medium High

BLOOD FLOW: Really Light Light Medium Heavy Really Heavy

NOTES

YOU
GOT
THIS !

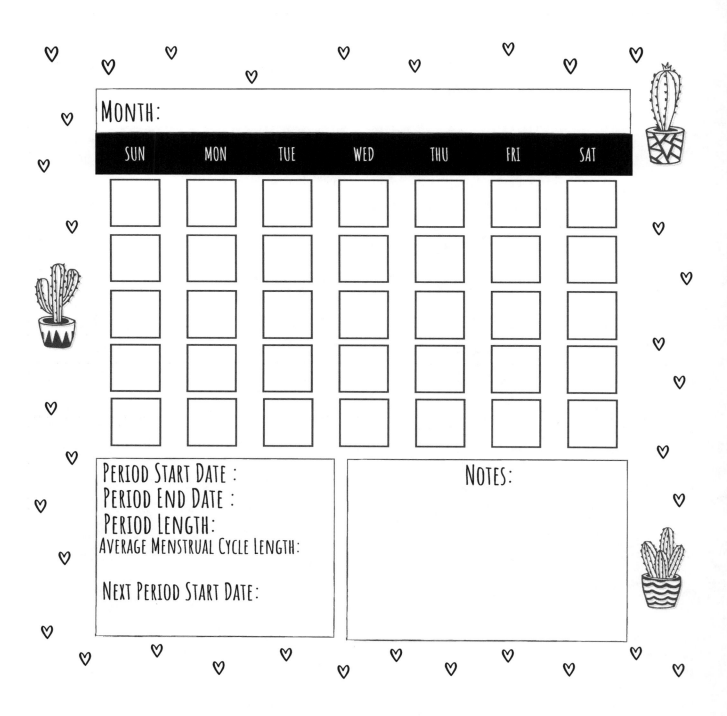

Month:

SUN	MON	TUE	WED	THU	FRI	SAT

Period Start Date :
Period End Date :
Period Length:
Average Menstrual Cycle Length:

Next Period Start Date:

Notes:

DATE:

MOOD: Sad Cranky Irritable Annoyed Happy Frustrated Tired Other:

SYMPTOMS: Cramps Sore Breast Headache Acne Bloating Other:

ENERGY Low Medium High

BLOOD FLOW: Really Light Light Medium Heavy Really Heavy

NOTES

DATE:

MOOD: Sad Cranky Irritable Annoyed Happy Frustrated Tired Other:

SYMPTOMS: Cramps Sore Breast Headache Acne Bloating Other:

ENERGY Low Medium High

BLOOD FLOW: Really Light Light Medium Heavy Really Heavy

NOTES

DATE:

MOOD: Sad Cranky Irritable Annoyed Happy Frustrated Tired Other:

SYMPTOMS: Cramps Sore Breast Headache Acne Bloating Other:

ENERGY Low Medium High

BLOOD FLOW: Really Light Light Medium Heavy Really Heavy

NOTES

DATE:

MOOD: Sad Cranky Irritable Annoyed Happy Frustrated Tired Other:

SYMPTOMS: Cramps Sore Breast Headache Acne Bloating Other:

ENERGY Low Medium High

BLOOD FLOW: Really Light Light Medium Heavy Really Heavy

NOTES

Date:

Mood: Sad Cranky Irritable Annoyed Happy Frustrated Tired Other:

Symptoms: Cramps Sore Breast Headache Acne Bloating Other:

Energy Low Medium High

Blood Flow: Really Light Light Medium Heavy Really Heavy

Notes

Date:

Mood: Sad Cranky Irritable Annoyed Happy Frustrated Tired Other:

Symptoms: Cramps Sore Breast Headache Acne Bloating Other:

Energy Low Medium High

Blood Flow: Really Light Light Medium Heavy Really Heavy

Notes

DATE:

MOOD: Sad   Cranky   Irritable   Annoyed   Happy   Frustrated   Tired   Other:

SYMPTOMS: Cramps   Sore Breast   Headache   Acne   Bloating   Other:

ENERGY   Low   Medium   High

BLOOD FLOW: Really Light   Light   Medium   Heavy   Really Heavy

NOTES

DATE:

MOOD: Sad   Cranky   Irritable   Annoyed   Happy   Frustrated   Tired   Other:

SYMPTOMS: Cramps   Sore Breast   Headache   Acne   Bloating   Other:

ENERGY   Low   Medium   High

BLOOD FLOW: Really Light   Light   Medium   Heavy   Really Heavy

NOTES

KEEP UP THE GOOD WORK!

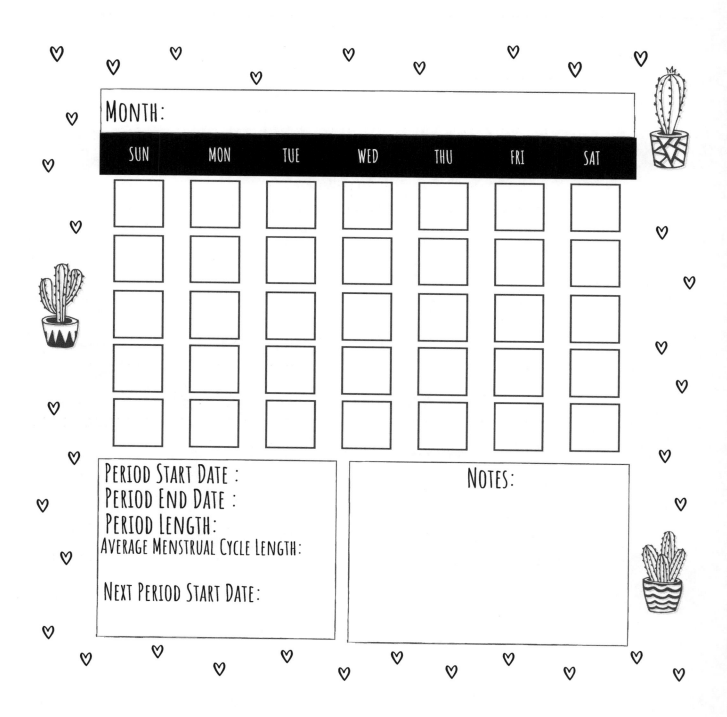

MONTH:

SUN	MON	TUE	WED	THU	FRI	SAT

PERIOD START DATE :
PERIOD END DATE :
PERIOD LENGTH:
AVERAGE MENSTRUAL CYCLE LENGTH:

NEXT PERIOD START DATE:

NOTES:

Date:

Mood: Sad Cranky Irritable Annoyed Happy Frustrated Tired Other:

Symptoms: Cramps Sore Breast Headache Acne Bloating Other:

Energy Low Medium High

Blood Flow: Really Light Light Medium Heavy Really Heavy

Notes

Date:

Mood: Sad Cranky Irritable Annoyed Happy Frustrated Tired Other:

Symptoms: Cramps Sore Breast Headache Acne Bloating Other:

Energy Low Medium High

Blood Flow: Really Light Light Medium Heavy Really Heavy

Notes

Date:

Mood: Sad Cranky Irritable Annoyed Happy Frustrated Tired   Other:

Symptoms: Cramps Sore Breast Headache Acne Bloating   Other:

Energy   Low Medium High

Blood Flow: Really Light Light Medium Heavy Really Heavy

Notes

Date:

Mood: Sad Cranky Irritable Annoyed Happy Frustrated Tired   Other:

Symptoms: Cramps Sore Breast Headache Acne Bloating   Other:

Energy   Low Medium High

Blood Flow: Really Light Light Medium Heavy Really Heavy

Notes

Date:

Mood: Sad Cranky Irritable Annoyed Happy Frustrated Tired Other:

Symptoms: Cramps Sore Breast Headache Acne Bloating Other:

Energy Low Medium High

Blood Flow: Really Light Light Medium Heavy Really Heavy

Notes

Date:

Mood: Sad Cranky Irritable Annoyed Happy Frustrated Tired Other:

Symptoms: Cramps Sore Breast Headache Acne Bloating Other:

Energy Low Medium High

Blood Flow: Really Light Light Medium Heavy Really Heavy

Notes

Date:

Mood: Sad Cranky Irritable Annoyed Happy Frustrated Tired Other:

Symptoms: Cramps Sore Breast Headache Acne Bloating Other:

Energy Low Medium High

Blood Flow: Really Light Light Medium Heavy Really Heavy

Notes

Date:

Mood: Sad Cranky Irritable Annoyed Happy Frustrated Tired Other:

Symptoms: Cramps Sore Breast Headache Acne Bloating Other:

Energy Low Medium High

Blood Flow: Really Light Light Medium Heavy Really Heavy

Notes

GREAT JOB! YOU HAVE TRACKED FOR 14 MONTHS!

MONTH:

SUN	MON	TUE	WED	THU	FRI	SAT

PERIOD START DATE :
PERIOD END DATE :
PERIOD LENGTH:
AVERAGE MENSTRUAL CYCLE LENGTH:

NEXT PERIOD START DATE:

NOTES:

Date:

Mood: Sad Cranky Irritable Annoyed Happy Frustrated Tired Other:

Symptoms: Cramps Sore Breast Headache Acne Bloating Other:

Energy Low Medium High

Blood Flow: Really Light Light Medium Heavy Really Heavy

Notes

Date:

Mood: Sad Cranky Irritable Annoyed Happy Frustrated Tired Other:

Symptoms: Cramps Sore Breast Headache Acne Bloating Other:

Energy Low Medium High

Blood Flow: Really Light Light Medium Heavy Really Heavy

Notes

Date:

Mood: Sad Cranky Irritable Annoyed Happy Frustrated Tired Other:

Symptoms: Cramps Sore Breast Headache Acne Bloating Other:

Energy Low Medium High

Blood Flow: Really Light Light Medium Heavy Really Heavy

Notes

Date:

Mood: Sad Cranky Irritable Annoyed Happy Frustrated Tired Other:

Symptoms: Cramps Sore Breast Headache Acne Bloating Other:

Energy Low Medium High

Blood Flow: Really Light Light Medium Heavy Really Heavy

Notes

DATE:

MOOD: Sad Cranky Irritable Annoyed Happy Frustrated Tired Other:

SYMPTOMS: Cramps Sore Breast Headache Acne Bloating Other:

ENERGY Low Medium High

BLOOD FLOW: Really Light Light Medium Heavy Really Heavy

NOTES

DATE:

MOOD: Sad Cranky Irritable Annoyed Happy Frustrated Tired Other:

SYMPTOMS: Cramps Sore Breast Headache Acne Bloating Other:

ENERGY Low Medium High

BLOOD FLOW: Really Light Light Medium Heavy Really Heavy

NOTES

Date:

Mood: Sad Cranky Irritable Annoyed Happy Frustrated Tired Other:

Symptoms: Cramps Sore Breast Headache Acne Bloating Other:

Energy Low Medium High

Blood Flow: Really Light Light Medium Heavy Really Heavy

Notes

Date:

Mood: Sad Cranky Irritable Annoyed Happy Frustrated Tired Other:

Symptoms: Cramps Sore Breast Headache Acne Bloating Other:

Energy Low Medium High

Blood Flow: Really Light Light Medium Heavy Really Heavy

Notes

DATE:

MOOD: Sad Cranky Irritable Annoyed Happy Frustrated Tired Other:

SYMPTOMS: Cramps Sore Breast Headache Acne Bloating Other:

ENERGY Low Medium High

BLOOD FLOW: Really Light Light Medium Heavy Really Heavy

NOTES

DATE:

MOOD: Sad Cranky Irritable Annoyed Happy Frustrated Tired Other:

SYMPTOMS: Cramps Sore Breast Headache Acne Bloating Other:

ENERGY Low Medium High

BLOOD FLOW: Really Light Light Medium Heavy Really Heavy

NOTES

Made in the USA
Las Vegas, NV
22 February 2023